The Complete S

The Crocodile! The Eagle...

A Ruthless Combination

By

Dr Ernest M Kadembo, Professor

Author of

Effective Prayers for Extraordinary Results

You can do the Impossible with God

The Key Code of Answered prayer

Story it! Brand it! Sell it!

Co-author of

The power of night prayers and divine encounters

© **Ernest Kadembo, 2017**

Inspired Transformations (Pvt) Ltd

We are those who inspire individuals and organizations through storytelling or re-story for excellence.

Website: www.inspiredtrans.com

Email: info@inspiredtrans.com

           ekadembo@yahoo.com

Phone: 00447949872265 / 0447710989048

Dedication

Dedicated to the many people who dare to live their dreams...yesterday, today and tomorrow. They have taken steps to change the world. Some made it big, others could not realise their dream...but they took a step. I salute your courage and efforts to give humanity something valuable. Whatever the outcomes of the efforts or steps they took, have taken or will take, there are many lessons for humanity from those daring efforts. Good or bad, bold decisions present lessons for those willing to learn.

Humanity owes it to them that initiatives and breakthroughs came forth and have inspired many to run with the gauntlet. The state of the world is an array of testimonies of many who took the leap for greatness or made to pioneer and did something that humanity can use, see or be inspired by and there are billions of such things, tangible and intangible. Whatever item, process or solution that has come into existence is an expression of man's adventure in contributing to humanity. I want to pay tribute to all the various instrumental people who have made a difference to humanity in different ways.

TRIBUTE TO THE LATE PROFESSOR PRIMROSE KURASHA, VC, ZOU

I am at a loss for the passing on of VC of ZOU, Prof Primrose Kurasha. The family, the academic fraternity and the nation of Zimbabwe have been robbed of one of a kind. It is no mean achievement to become a vice chancellor of a university.

That loss saddens me but the association I had with her gives me pride that I could call on her. I called her my mother, my teacher, my colleague and my friend. We grew in faith and encouraged each other. The Lord was faithful in her tribulations and she could testify the goodness of the Lord. She witnessed the workings of God in her life and formed the cloud of witnesses referred to in Hebrews 12: 1. In her last few days before passing on shewas inspiring me with spiritually enriching messages, the last one being on 11 February 2017, siix days before her passing on. That was really empowering. She enriched me academically, she was with me in challenges and she was a pillar of the Harare 2016 Strategy & Marketing Indaba as a speaker and distinguished delegate.

In your passing on madam I salute you as a master, a leader and an inspiration. I am forever, grateful that grace brought us together for the transformation we have enjoyed. To mudhara wangu, Prof Jameson Kurasha and the girls you are not alone. We grieve together and seek grace. Our prayers shall always be with you.

May the soul of Prof Primrose Kurasha RIP.

Prof. Ernest M Kadembo

About the Author

Dr Ernest Kadembo is a professor of business, an academic with diverse interests and experience stretching nearly thirty years cutting across Zimbabwe and the United Kingdom. He is well travelled and enjoys a global network of associates. His areas of expertise include strategy, marketing, quality, branding, story branding, change management, leadership, international business, among many other areas of expertise. Ernest is a career academic who thanks God for favour in attaining a range of qualifications in the area of Business Management. He holds a PhD in Story branding, an MBA (Marketing), an MSc Information Systems Management, an Honours degree in Business Studies, a Postgraduate Certificate in Education, a certificate in E-Moderation (online teaching) and a certificate in International Marketing Case Writing. Dr Kadembo's PhD is on *The Storytelling approach in in developing a brand*.

These qualifications mean nothing without the grace of God and he thanks God who has granted him these qualifications and an array of opportunities. Dr Kadembo dreams of establishing a huge presence on the global arena as an expert in story branding, management and marketing. As already alluded to, he would treasure using this influence and expertise to extend the kingdom agenda wherever he gets involved in training and consultancy in his areas of expertise. Professor Kadembo has made significant contribution to the Kingdom agenda as a prayer warrior, preacher and teacher. He derives his mandate from various divine encounters.

As the convener and chief strategist of the Strategy & Marketing Think Tank Forum Dr Kadembo is confident he can be a catalyst in business excellence and innovation to individuals and business.

Content

Dedication		-3-
Tribute to the Late Professor Primrose Kurasha, VC Zimbabwe Open University		-4-
About the author		- 6-
Content		- 8-
Preface		- 9-
Chapter 1	Introduction	-12-
Chapter 2	The Essence of Strategy	-20-
Chapter 3	The Strategy Process	-32-
Chapter 4	Strategy and Change	-56-
Chapter 5	Leadership and Strategy	-68-
Chapter 6	The Strategic Mind of the Eagle	-85-
Chapter 7	The Strategic Mind of the Crocodile	-92-
Chapter 8	The Strategic Mind of the Snake	-98-
Chapter 9	The Complete Strategic Mindset	-103-
Chapter 10	Stop Dreaming! Act Now	-127-
	References	-136-

Preface

The strategic thought process is critical in championing the direction an organisation takes in realising its mission, vision and objectives. Individuals and organisations from every walk of life have a strategy for sustenance, whether explicitly stated or implied. The notion of strategy has been hyped as a complicated process often seen as a preserve for large organisations. But, the reality of strategy is more mundane and simpler to contextualise to every engagement in advancing an agenda for any individual, group or organisation.

Put simply, every effort to realise objectives amounts to a strategy. That process can be complicated or simple depending on the task at hand. The practice and praxis of strategy can be deliberate and consciously done, which is about formulation, or could be an accumulation of incremental decisions often termed muddling through or strategy formation. Participants in the process of strategy are at various levels of the organisational hierarchy. Strategy is often attributed to the corporate level of the organisation, but the reality is that it occurs across every level of the organisational hierarch and differs in the scope of engagement at the different levels. The difference in strategy involvement are epitomised in the complexity and breadth of responsibility and accountability of the team or incumbent at the respective levels.

The fact that we all engage in strategy in whatever we do does not make everyone a strategist. There are many things we do in everyday life, like playing sport as a hobby, not as a profession; that does not make us experts in doing them. Every practice or discipline demands a certain mindset and principles to enhance execution for that practice. The idea of a strategy is quite intriguing as it shapes the destiny of an individual or organisation. If the strategy does not address the situation at hand the organisation goes off course. It will veer off on a trajectory that sets off at a tangent and miss the target.

The idea of a complete strategic mindset has a broad perspective of the dynamics of how an organisation negotiates its way in a complex world of business with multitudes of competing individuals and organisations. True strategic thinking demands a winning mentality and the staying power to withstand the competitor moves from the dynamic environment. Strategic thinking requires adapting to situations and also initiating moves that will give an advantage over the competition. It is a commonality that organisational success depends on the way an organisation meets its set out objectives; that is its strategy.

Whether it is about how we nourish our bodies, develop ourselves, run organisations, defend ourselves or protect ourselves, we need a strategy to realise the objectives set out. Whether by instinct or through professional development there is need to craft a strategy for meeting the expected results. This book calls for a mindset that deals with the big picture and its challenges; hence the title, *The Complete Strategic Mindset! The Eagle! The Crocodile! The Snake! It is a Ruthless Combination.*

Chapter 1

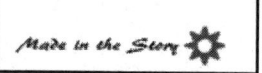

Introduction

Dare to be a Winner

In pursuing an understanding of the fundamentals of strategy, there is a need for an open mind to be able to conceptualise the big picture. The related thought processes and positioning are critical as the complete strategic mindset takes one to the top of the game. In that regard, we should realise that to be strategic minded one should be outstanding in what he/she does or their organisation is aware of how to play the game in a defined terrain. Crafting an appropriate winning strategy requires that the strategist understands the environmental forces at play which impact organisational performance in order to align the organisation in an effective manner.

Given that strategy is about the big picture and having foresight of the broad direction it is imperative that those involved are visionary and analytical. This necessitates a futuristic perspective focused on connecting to a destiny clearly thought out in the form of a vision. That perspective and posture demand a critical and imaginative mindset that analyses the present and connect to a future that an organisation can plan for and have a dominant position when that future arrives. It follows that a complete strategic mindset has characteristics which border on being at the top of the game. This amounts to a mentality and action which will put the organisation a step ahead of other players:

    Will outdo
    Will outwit
    Will outpace
    Will outclass
    Will outmanoeuvre
    Will outshine
    Will outsmart
    Will outlive
    Will outperform

The essence of a strategic mindset projects a player who is ahead of the game. Individuals and organisations should capture the momentum of the times within the paradigm of the moment and charter a path to the top. The complete strategic mindset can relate with yesterday, today and tomorrow and connects to the wave of the moment to be a winner. Individuals and organisations with a strategic mindset are imaginative in their approach and their agendas are creative and progressive. Etzold (2009) says that: "But acting strategically means not allowing yourself to be discouraged by setbacks." The complete strategic thinker has a total approach, ie., creative, imaginative, dynamic, critical and above all sensitive to the challenges in the environment. Failure is momentary and is an opportunity to try something different. The legendary USA basketball player Michael Jordan says that he is a success because he failed many times. There can never be radical change or impact caused without going through the lessons of failure to improve the next step. Many people with a lot of potential to excel cannot withstand the true ~~ for excellence because they see a setback as the end. Instead, a setback should be viewed as an opportunity to improve or to learn some things to avoid the next time of trying.

The meaning of Strategy

The notion of strategy is about meeting objectives of an organisation. It is important to remind the reader that organisations are human contrived institutions; hence people make organisations tick through their concerted efforts, imagination, creativity and thinking. In simple terms, strategy is about the means to an end. Henry Minzberg, a management guru submits different perspectives on how to view strategy; suggesting that a strategy could be seen as a *plan, a pattern, a plot, a perspective or a position.*

A *plan* suggests determining a future course of action in advance; ie, walking in the future before that future unfolds. A *pattern* shows a path or an approach that takes a certain shape in doing things over time. A *plot* implies moves to outwit and beat the opposition in the course of time. This connotes that strategy entails fighting for space in the business environment. A *perspective* presents strategy as a way of looking at a situation or an approach to directing an organisation towards fulfilling its mission, vision and objectives. The last view of strategy taken by Minzberg is strategy as a *position,* which points at strategy as a relative posture in the dynamics of the competitive arena.

By presenting these different views on strategy it helps readers and practitioners realise that there are different ways of looking at the phenomenon of strategy and the related thought processes. What matters most in looking at strategy is the idea of acting to meet the set out objectives of an organisation or an individual.

Why Strategy

It may not sound obvious, but the key issue in underpinning strategy is the realisation of objectives. That places the strategy as a means of meeting the objectives and the mission of the organisation. Ultimately, strategy answers the question: *How do we get there?* This phenomenon is not limited to business but also to organisations or animals in a survival mode or in a fight to control space or dominate the players in a given domain. There are many situations where strategy matters in different human functionalities. In sports, the strategy is crucial in order to win against the opposition. In the case of sport or in a fight the focus is on beating the opponent. In every engagement in a sport or military situation there is a need to balance the offensive and the defensive approaches. The idea is to score and avoid giving away chances to the opposition and concede goals.

Every confrontation in combat or business calls for two key actions. As much as one seeks to score they would also want to avoid conceding to the opponent. The baseline in strategy and in sport is attack and defence. There has to be a balance between the two aspects of realising strategy and winning against competition. The key is to fight from one's strengths.

There has to be a balance on how and when to attack while protecting the back. Using an analogy of football, it is not often that teams will attack and defend with the same intensity. Some teams are more attacking minded while others are more defensive in their approach. Either, strategy will suffice depending on the resources available; hence teams with more attacking flair would employ their fluidity in attack as a defence, hence they defend from the front. On the other hand more tackling teams that win balls would build a defensive wall and counteract the offensive flair of the opponent.

Strategy is inescapable or in other terms, it is ubiquitous, that is, it is present in every situation. Whenever something needs to be achieved it necessitates developing or pursuing a certain strategy. The study of strategy at the pinnacle of learning, in higher institutions of learning has created a misnomer that strategy is elitist. Animals employ strategies in meeting their objectives, be it in a fight within the family or hunting prey. The big issue is about how to win. Ultimately survival demands a strategy; just like in the jungle, either the prey outruns the hunter or the hunter catches the prey. In everyday life the challenge to win against competition presents a situation similar to jungle life.

People and organisations need to meet objectives in a simple or complex setting and that attracts strategies to make a difference. While strategy is a necessity in meeting objectives or as a mode for survival, it is important to note that the process could be an outcome of chance rather than a deliberate process that is well thought out. However, the ideal approach would be to plan the strategy methodically and implement it. To assume that strategy will work out well by chance is tantamount to suggest that strategy evolves on its own. Given that at the core of strategy is a plan it is imperative to provide a clearly thought out framework for future moves and directions. The means to realise the objectives underpin the strategy of the organisation. Therefore, a logical approach to developing a strategy would mean thinking through the objectives and linking them to the strategy process. Ultimately strategy will determine winning or losing in a given operational space and charter the long-term prospects of the organisation.

Chapter 2

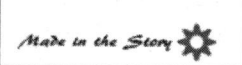

The Essence of Strategy

Understanding Strategy

The strategy for a given situation provides the direction an organisation takes when pursuing a mission, vision and objectives to shape the agenda of the organisation. Put in a simple way, strategy refers to: A range or set of goal-directed decisions and actions matching an organization's skills and resources with the opportunities and threats in its environment and aligning them to the environment in a beneficial manner.

It is imperative that strategy captures the forces of the environment at work and operate to maximise performance in that context. It is clear from the submissions that the essence of strategy is epitomised in applying resources to the dynamics of the environment. Ultimately the arguments that are crucial to understanding the essence of strategy, embrace the process of how to make the strategic vision a reality and achieve target objectives set out by the organisation. The issues pertaining to strategy and strategic management require a clear understanding of the forces at play within the organisation and without. Effective strategy development requires a deeper understanding of the forces that impact on the realisation of objectives and creating a dominant market position. In developing the strategy, it is critical that the right questions are asked about the meaning and critical decisions that are made in respect of the strategy. When those questions are asked, it is easy to shape the strategies in the right manner.

The Key Questions

The notion of strategy seeks to address fundamental questions about an organisation's standing in the advancement of its mission, vision and objectives. It is imperative that if strategy is to guide an organisation towards meeting its objectives, it becomes critical to answer a number of questions that shape the thinking towards meeting the demands of a strategy.

The six key questions form the foundation of the strategic thought process and techniques. The six questions are about *Where, What, When, How, Why and Who*. Strategic thinking and planning needs to give comprehensive scrutiny to the internal and external environmental dynamics. The critical questions about the strategic thought process would encompass the specific questions set out in the subsequent sections.

The question on who we are puts the individual or organisation into the right posture – whether an SME, a conglomerate, a multinational or any other type of organisation operating in a defined context. Oftentimes individuals and organisations daydream about who they are and where they are going. It is important to be realistic about the strategic posture in respect of capabilities, context and other essential traits and resources that facilitate the execution of strategies if strategies are to be effective. Not being realistic in looking at onself is as good as denying one's identity as reflected in a mirror. With that kind of attitude we end up dealing with falsehoods, instead of the reality of our circimstances.

a. **Who are we?**

This draws on the organisation's standing, ie., the purpose for existence. This question helps define the mission of the organisation, the generic need fulfilled by the organisation. Often this is mistaken for the means instead of the solution provided. Airline companies, bus companies and train services are not in the business of their technology, but are a provider of transport services using different means. That perspective means that the strategist will look at other players utilising different technologies as competitors. Strategic thinking is comprehensive and holistic which would necessitate a plan that takes into account the different players with a view to shape a clear identity to compete in the market. The key to success lies in developing a practical and realistic broad plan to beneficially align with the environment. Competition in business can be complex and diverse and would require a robust stance in dealing with the various issues.

b.   Where are we?

This is self introspection where an organisation seeks to evaluate the current state of the business or individual posture relative to the direction being taken. If one is to move in any direction towards a destination that move is relative to the current position which becomes the starting point. If a company is operating in one region of a country with an intention to enter other regions that defines its position. That position is relative to the environmental dynamics. In that regard, the strategic position is epitomised in environmental analysis. That process takes into cognisance the internal and external dynamics of the organisation. Ultimately, the environmental analysis yields a profile of factors internal and external to the organisation. The internal analysis will provide strengths and weaknesses of the organisation, while the external analysis provides a profile of opportunities and threats. A combination of the outcomes of the internal and external analysis is summarised in the SWOT (representing the Strengths, Weaknesses, Opportunities and Threats).

c. **Where do we want to be?**

This question projects the future the organisation envisages itself in. This aspect of strategy encapsulates the vision and other related fundamentals of the organisation that underpin the future position the organisation seeks to realise. Objectives are shaped around this question, and that includes the long-term and short-term objectives. The idea is to project a future desired state which the organisation is gunning for. The main issues under consideration will be market position, volume of business, competitive position, the model of doing business, extent of expansion within and without amongst many other issues.

The vision provides a long term perspective for a future state or watershed, which underpins a state of achievement. Essentially, the question of where to is a futuristic mental picture of the business' direction. That posture provides a mental frame of where the organisation is headed. That is what is often termed the vision of the organisation. Too often the term vision has been used in circumstances attributable to confusion and daydreaming. This mixed picture is quite common with both organisations and individuals. A vision should provide a clear posture of a future desired state of attainment. This is not tantamount to guessing or simply raising a thump and suggesting it is done. The reality of a vision is epitomised in a clear sense of direction with potential to be attained moving from a defined position. The thought process and the practical steps to be taken need to be thought through instead of engaging in sweet nothings and empty platitudes. There must be a realistic chance of attainment with a roadmap conceptualised to realise that vision.

d.   How do we get there?

Every aspiration necessitates an approach to realise it, otherwise the plans remain a pipe dream. Strategy is the means to realise the vision and objectives. The *How* of meeting those objectives is not a universal approach because the approach has to fit the prevailing circumstances, that is the internal and external environment forces at play. The right strategy seeks to beneficially align the organisation with the environment and it is not something that can be easily copied. The strategy is determined by objectives at hand and the environmental dynamics. It is important that the respective strategies are focused on the vision and objectives set out, but also responsive to the forces of the environment. The approach taken in dealing with any issue needs to consider the objectives to be met and prevailing circumstances.

Every strategy should mirror both the aspirations and available resources, both human and material. The how of strategy is critical because it is a reality check about whether we can do what we claim or not. Often the question to leaders about how they will meet their claims invokes anger and arrogance because most people do not want to be real as they cannot justify their plans. We cannot wish our way to success without being real. The idea of politicking with business does not work. We cannot just tell everyone that it will work when there is no plan nor resources or simply ignore the need for resources while sounding idealistic.

e.   When do we get there?

In management planning time is a key consideration as a measure of performance and productivity. It is therefore critical to harness the element of time in shaping the range of activities. While some strategies might be appropriate in meeting the objectives the timing might be wrong and therefore reduce the impact of the strategic moves. Time is a resource that needs to be managed effectively and every second that ticks costs money to the organisation hence failure to perform is a leakage that amounts to a loss to the organisation. Given that objectives are timed; it is extremely important that schedules and targets are met as planned. Productivity is also measured as output per given time. If an organisation sets out to achieve something and does not put a time frame that means there is no point at which a review should question whether or not such objectives would have been achieved.

The time value of money cannot be ignored in the ultimate assessment or measurement of performance. Every measurement of performance requires a time dimension and therefore, the strategic planning process and assessment of performance necessitate a time dimension. In the developing world, attitudes towards time must change if progress is to be made in negotiations and task performance.

f.   Who does it?

Every act in business does not happen on its own nor is it a matter of serendipity; which is a chance happening. At the core of organisational performance is responsibility and accountability for individuals or groups for the task(s) to be executed. The framework for organising the execution of plans necessitates a structure within which to operationalise business activities. There is a hierarchy of authority that allows for the flow of command and control. At the same time the flow of information follows the hierarchical structure in terms of the reporting of performance. Where performance is not in line with the plan the control systems will also utilise the structures which define the centres of responsibility and accountability. Those evaluations of performance will also facilitate reward systems for motivating performance and also shape parameters of standards of performance.

There are many fundamental elements that need consideration when coming up with an organisational structure in shaping an organisation. The nature of the task at hand, the industry dynamics and the culture of the organisation are taken into consideration when determining a structure. The generic approaches include functional structures, divisional and matrix structures. The different structures suit different circumstances and there is need for a reflective evaluation of what works for the organisation.

Chapter 3

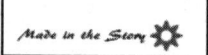

The Strategy Process

Introduction

Strategy refers to a plan for how to achieve a given objective(s). While every act of meeting a set of objectives could be referred to as a strategy the common understanding is that strategy is a long term and broad in approach covering the whole organisation. The idea is to exploit the opportunities facing the organisation and beneficially align with the environment. The academic dogma appears to suggest a systematic process, but the reality is that strategy can be formal or informal and can still achieve the desired objectives. At the same time it is important to note that strategy takes place at different levels of the organisation; *operations* at the frontline; *tactics* or *stratagems* at middle management or supervisory levels and *strategy* at business and corporate levels. The corporate strategy cascades downwards to lower levels of the organisation for ease of implementation and accountability. The higher the level of the strategic threshold on the corporate hierarchy the longer the horizon for the time frame of the strategy.

Process refers to the steps undertaken to complete a given task or meet a set of objectives. Many authors have advanced the notion of strategy and present the respective stages an organisation undergoes in order to develop one and execute it. In the academic discourse on strategy we often talk about paralysis by analysis, the notion that so much time is expended in trying to understand situations and drowning in the search for understanding the phenomenon without getting to the point of deciding or acting. As already alluded to, the idea of a strategy is an answer to "How is it done or How do we get there?"

In making the notion of strategy sound simple is the trigger for success in developing and implementing strategies. The idea is for the strategy to be simple enough to understand and make it easier to implement. Sometimes strategies are made complicated by the jargon employed to make things look professional and sophisticated. But, the whole purpose of strategy demands creating a sense of mission across the whole organisation so that everyone knows the path to follow and would not need force to perform as expected. People do more when they understand the reasons for doing something.

Ultimately, strategy simply demands that the responsible personnel "Just do the right thing". In this chapter the idea is to demonstrate in simple terms what it takes to be focused and act to get results. Sometimes we use the term "The end justifies the means." There are many who would say we need morals in operationalising the processes. That I totally agree, but sometimes things have to be done through a painful process no matter what. A pregnant woman will deliver through a cesarean section when circumstances make it impossible to do a natural delivery. Life is not always ideal. Some people have had to die while fighting for freedom even though there could have been negotiations but someone decided to be stubborn and intransigent. The strategy to win freedom moves from mutual negotiation to confrontation and violence depending on the opposition in the confrontation.

The Nature of Strategy Development

While the notion of strategy has been explained as an answer to "How to meet objectives or get a result" the reality is that developing a strategy is not a standard conventional process. There are many people who are pursuing a strategy without knowing it is a strategy and the same applies to animals like lions hunting prey. The idea of a strategy is about *thinking and action*. That balance is important in strategy. The logic in this submission is that oftentimes strategies are not even documented.

Some strategies are a pattern shaped in the range of activities undertaken in championing a destiny. The academic jargon refers to this as muddling through or logical incrementalism and tends to be referred to as strategy formation. In that regard strategy emerges from a process of many decisions and actions that provide a pattern and that process is referred to as *strategy formation*. Therefore, we can still have a strategy without sitting down to develop one. Actually we can have a strategy without knowing it is a strategy, let alone ever seen or read a book about the notion of strategy. So the how to is universal and does not discriminate on background knowledge or specie. The refinement in the approach will distinguish champions from the also runs in strategic thinking and implementation.

If someone was driving a car and it developed a problem leading to malfunction that necessitates a strategy to fix it. If the problem meant that the car could still drive; a cautious diver could drive on the extreme lane used by slow-moving cars and switch on hazard waening lights to inform other motorists as the car slowly crawls down the road. One could still reach their destination later than planned, but still manages to meet the objective of getting to the destination. The strategy in this case is driving slowly on the slow drivers' lane. So ultimately we can ascertain that we can all engage in strategy at different thresholds; sometimes as ignorant people completely devoid of knowledge, novices trying to get to grips with issues or experts who calculate their moves. There is an element of common sense and instinct in pursuing the basic survival strategies.

In showing that the development and execution of a strategy does not necessarily require one to know what strategy means nor formally develop it, does not nullify the need for understanding and formally developing strategy. Just like with all aspects of human functionality we are better off with a formal approach and sound understanding of the fundamental concepts. I had the pleasure of brushing shoulders with a seasoned entrepreneur who said that: "The reason for education in entrepreneurship is to avoid the thorns that those who engaged in the process without education suffered." This submission holds sway on the need for learning about and developing a strategy. Basic knowledge used without proper appreciation can be disastrous, it is important to understand before taking steps. Many people who could do very little swimming on the shallow end died trying to venture on the deep end before they were well prepared to go to the deep end.

Whenever possible, it is better to grasp the concept before attempting to do something. I have seen enough gadgets broken by people who never read the instructions and acted with little information but keen on imagination about how the gadget works. Many battles have been lost because of zeal without logic. In extreme circumstances sometimes people may act in desperation and get a result; let not that be considered the rule because it is the exception. There are many people who seem to be driven by the desire to gamble their way to stardom. That mentality has limited chances for success. A more resolute and assured approach is better than plunging into darkness, hoping that light shall shine, but there is never any light in some tunnels and disaster awaits.

There are thousands of management and business departments in universities, private colleges, business schools, consulting organisation among multitudes of other institutions which specialise in developing and teaching strategies. Those institutions are well subscribed and even after students have complete respective studies there is still more exposure through online resources and print material to update on knowledge about strategy and the shift in strategic thinking over time. Internal programmes are in place to facilitate learning and development of strategic thinking. Strategy has become so important to business to sound like a religious ritual without which business practice is inadequate. Despite all the focus and resources committed to strategy development and execution organisations still fail. Strategy or the notion of planning in its generic sense is not a panacea for success. The routine process is not enough; equally important is the need for creative thinking and decisive action. The right thinking and the right plan can still fail if the implementation does not match the plan.

In articulating these critical views I intend to make it clear that while strategy can be a simple process that does not render it simplistic. Ultimately, the strategy becomes one of the main determining factors for success in doing something especially in business. The basic tenet in business is to know where one is going just as the popular saying in management would go: "If you don't know where you are going any road will take there; or "If you don't know where you are going how do you know you are there?" Another common truism often echoed in management is that: "To manage business is to manage information." Once more the need to know is highlighted. This is the reason why institutions invest vast amounts of resources to learn about strategy and execute it.

Organisations with a formal approach to strategy will create the right platform to educate people and develop the strategy. Having discussed the informal or subconscious practices in strategy the focus now shifts to the formal approach. The various institutions and consultants who train and advise on strategy development are guided by a set of principles and employ a process to perform the strategy process.

This book is not an academic book and will not attempt to sound theoretical. The arguments put forward provide a simple and realistic approach to strategic thinking and implementation. Ultimately, any practitioner wishing to develop strategic thinking, or develop and implement a strategy should be comfortable with the process. Since strategy is a corporate-wide process it demands that all parties that have a company-wide effect contribute to the process of developing the strategy. The key is to mutually concur on the broad direction. It is also fitting and proper to have that agreement across the senior management in the organisation because organisations by their nature operate through teams.

If the leadership or management team does not pull together there is potential for dysfunctional conflict where disagreements can be retrogressive and disruptive to the organisational ethos. Where an organisation formally institutes a process to engage as a management team, sometimes with the help of a consultant to develop a strategy, the process is referred to as *strategy formulation*. That process is conscious and deliberate and shapes the strategy of the organisation, determines implementation and control processes. In the academic jargon the complete process is referred to as strategic management. The various stages of the strategic management process are presented as follows:

Stage	Description	Purpose
Analysis	This stage looks into the state of the external and internal environments with a view to determining their effects on the standing of the organisation. Without understanding those fundamentals it is difficult to decide.	Underpins the external opportunities and threats and the internal strengths and weaknesses (SWOT).
Diagnosis	The diagnosis determines the main business elements and their implications to the broad direction that the organisation should take. These issues will underpin the organisation's core in terms of the broad direction and essence of business.	The business is defined in terms of its fundamentals such as mission, vision and objectives which define direction.
Choice/ Decision	This is the point at which options are determined and a selection is made on what would be the best way to go.	A strategy or strategies are chosen and agreed.
Implementation/Execution	This is the process of executing or putting the strategy into action. This is actually doing what would have been decided.	The strategy is put to action in order to meet objectives within a structure.
Control	This entails ensuring that the execution is consistent with the strategic plan. In other words the two should be in tandem.	Ensures that the strategy and the actual implementation match.

Understanding the Stages of Strategic Management

Having summarised what each stage makes it look quite simple. However, there is need to appreciate the finer detail expected in order to carry out each stage effectively. One should be quick to note that strategy is both a qualitative and quantitative process. Ultimately the strategy is realised within a budget. We cannot dream of doing everything and anything beyond our capabilities. Whatever decision is made on the objectives and the strategy to be embarked on the requisite resources in terms of the 5Ms as epitomised by machinery, money, manpower, management and materials are available to realise the strategy. However, over time there has been a realisation that 5Ms are not enough, instead there has to be an extra M making them 6 M. The sixth M is minutes or time. Everything should have a time dimension. Below, clarity is provided on the various stages of the strategic management process so that if one was to try and apply the process they will be able to make some sense of it.

Analysis

This stage is largely about trying to understand the forces at work within the organisation and without. Organisations do not operate like a self-sustaining island nor like an amoeba which does not depend on the external environment. An organisation is like a flowing river which receives water and in turn pours it somewhere. In the process the river is enriched by what it receives and in turn enriches the ocean it pours into. However, not everything around the river is good and what comes in does not necessarily equal what goes out of the river. In relating the logic to a business setup it is clear that organisations face opportunities from the external environment. These are situations that can be beneficially exploited, like an increase in disposable income in the market. At the same time if a competitor sets up business that brings a threat as it eats into the market share of the organisation. On the other hand where an organisation has a good position in its internal dynamics like having a healthy cash position that constitutes a strength which can be employed to exploit opportunities in the market. However, a situation where an organisation's workforce is well trained will present a weakness which may make it difficult to operate or withstand the forces in the environment. The analysis looks into a diverse range of factors relevant for the process of strategic planning (http://www.leoisaac.com/planning/strat016.ht).

These factors mirror the external and internal dynamics an organisation has to deal with, within its internal setup, in the micro and macro levels of its environment.

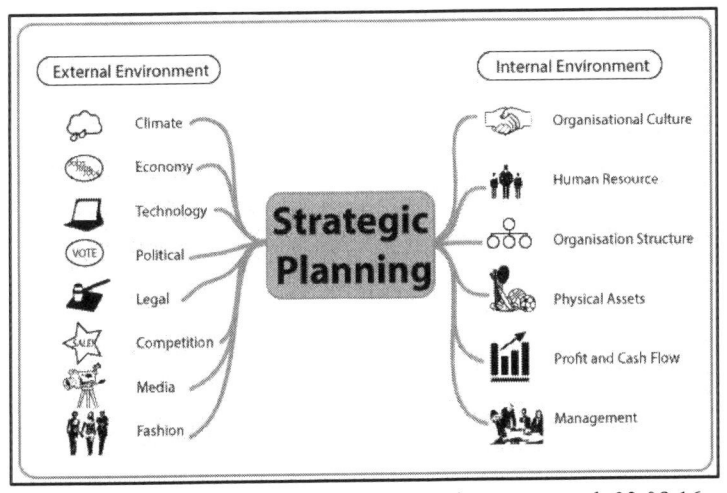

http://www.leoisaac.com/planning/strat016.htm; accessed, 03.08.16.

The external environment at macro level looks at many factors which include political/ legal, economic, technological, ecological and social factors. At the micro level the process looks at the competition, financial institutions, customers, labour unions, regulatory bodies etc. The micro forces are immediate to the organisation and they interact with the business on a regular basis. The external forces shape the opportunities and threats that an organisation faces from the external environment. The internal forces of the organisation underpin the strengths and weaknesses which define the organisation's capability to deal with the opportunities and threats it faces. At the heart of strategic planning is the interface of the forces in the environment represented by strengths, weaknesses, opportunities and threats, (SWOT).

Diagnosis

Diagnosis is a term often associated with the medical profession and would appear of little significance to management and strategy. However, that term is extremely important as it underpins the process of examining the state of the business and where it will be headed. Essentially the same ethos applies as in the medical situation. The strategist is looking at how healthy the organisation and what could be done to give the organisation life or how fit the organisation is.

In the case of strategic thinking the focus is on fundamental issues which define the core of the business as epitomised in the mission, vision and objectives. The mission defines what an organisation exists to serve, this is the benefit derived such as transport, health solutions, entertainment, etc. The problem in most cases is that organisations tend to focus on the means instead of the need or the benefit; airlines are not in the airline business but transport. The vision defines a watershed projected in the life of the organisation at a future point in time; something like; *landing a man on the moon by.., having a paperless office by.... having cyber space storage by ...or a desktop for every household by...* These are expressions of a leader who is seeing a certain futuristic posture for the organisation and rallies the leadership team and the organisation at large towards realising that dream. Martin Luther King spoke of his dream in the popular speech that became the rallying point for the advancement of Afro Americans, "I have a dream".

The vision is cascaded into objectives which progressively build towards the vision. Objectives are specific outcomes or results that an organisation undertakes to meet. Good objectives are specific, measurable, attainable, realistic and time-bound and are represented by the acronym SMART. In the organisation's ethos it is imperative that there is clarity on the direction and related objectives set out.

Choice/ Decision

At the heart of the management function is decision-making. The choice/decision stage of strategic management generates options in meeting the different objectives. The different options are evaluated in terms of feasibility; that is whether or not they are doable. The options should be acceptable to the stakeholders since without the commitment of the parties it is difficult to galvanise everyone's energy towards the organisation's agenda. Furthermore, consideration is given to the suitability of the strategy in the light of the prevailing environmental forces at play. Ultimately every strategy should be within the budgetary capabilities of the organisation. All the strategic choices fall into four categories:

a) Growth
b) Limited growth
c) Turnaround
d) Retrenchment

The growth strategy relates to expansion of a business embracing a range of approaches. On the other hand the limited growth entails stable expansion of the business. Turnaround relates to a change of direction or focus of the business. Retrenchment refers to closing shop or put another way getting out of a particular type of business.

Implementation/Execution

No matter how well a plan is crafted it does not

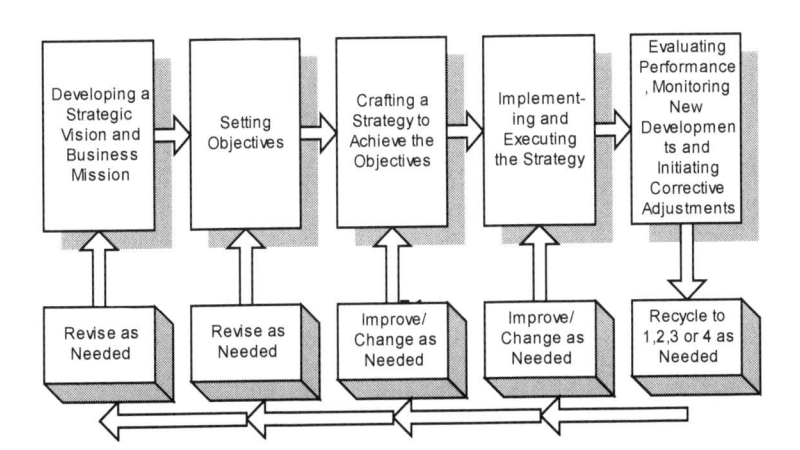

Developing a Strategic Vision and Business Mission	→	Setting Objectives	→	Crafting a Strategy to Achieve the Objectives	→	Implementing and Executing the Strategy	→	Evaluating Performance, Monitoring New Developments and Initiating Corrective Adjustments
↑		↑		↑		↑		↓
Revise as Needed		Revise as Needed		Improve/ Change as Needed		Improve/ Change as Needed		Recycle to 1,2,3 or 4 as Needed

make sense if that plan cannot be put to action, which is the implementation or execution of that plan or strategy. Whatever goes through the process of crafting strategies, ultimately someone should act on it. The implementation of a strategy should be timed over a horizon. That is necessary to ensure that there is a point to assess the degree of compliance with the way the strategy is operationalised and the extent to which it will be meeting objectives. It follows that effective implementation of strategy requires responsibility and accountability. Someone should take charge of the strategy, whether the overall strategy or the tactics that make-up the overall strategy.

Those who are tasked with responsibility will require a structure that provides the lines of authority for commands, the channelling of resources and information. Often organisations assume they could get results without a clear structure not appropriate resources as they tend to focus on satisfying certain stakeholders without being realistic about the demands of implementation.

The overall picture for implementation demands that the chief strategist in the form of the managing director, CEO or general manager, whichever title they carry are pragmatic in dealing with the situation. The resourcing gives consideration to the 6Ms as earlier alluded to. It is imperative to note that the trajectory of the strategy may shift as the situation unfolds because certain assumptions that form the basis of the decision making process may change as the environment changes. Therefore, effective strategy implementation necessitates flexibility in approach.

Evaluation and Control

When implementing a strategy there is no guarantee that whatever was planned will be realised as pre-determined. The expectation is to match the planned against the actual if the desired outcomes are to be achieved in the implementation of the strategy. For a variety of reasons the actual performance does not always match the planned. Sometimes the implementation itself is fraught with a variety of problems. As long as the actual execution is not in line with the plan that means neither the strategy nor the objectives are achieved. In order to ensure that the gap between the planned and the actual does not grow big there is need to monitor the implementation in line with the strategy. If there are any disparities between the two an evaluation to determine the reasons for the variation is carried out.

Once an evaluation of the implementation has been conducted the requisite corrective action is recommended. Ordinarily there are three ways of controlling the implementation of a strategy. Control takes the form of *predetermined control*; *in-process or steering control* and *feedback control*. The in-process control necessitates regular adjustments when the implementation is shifting away from the planned; the predetermined control is setting a red line like a budget for which a unity cannot spend more than allocated; and the feedback control is reviewing results periodically and comparing with the expected and taking relevant action.

The Continuous Cycle

Strategy is not an end in itself for every phase of implementation leads back to analysis and planning. Organisations never stop planning and implementation. It is imperative that organisations maintain a futuristic posture which necessitates regular reviews and adjustments to remain contemporary. As long as an organisation is a going concern strategic thinking, planning and implantation are mandatory.

Chapter 4

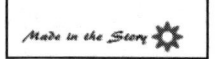

Strategy and Change

The Ubiquitous Nature of Change

The notion of strategy demands a regular review of the processes and systems that underpin the dynamics of the business environment and the new initiatives. Every strategy is anchored on the fundamental forces shaping the agenda and paradigm of the times.

Whether one believes in creation or evolution the thrust is that both phenomena set in motion the clock for change. As for creation God's calling of every entity to come into existence is a revolution that brought about phenomenal change that set in motion a vastly gigantic paradigm shift. On the other hand the evolutionary process underpins a gradual process of transformation. It therefore follows that from sunrise to sunset, every second, every minute, every hour, every day, every week, every month, every year, every decade, every generation and every century defines a turning point for change. These times define seasons for change and every turn of a period shapes a new momentum. Nothing lasts forever and therefore a mind stuck in yesterday's paradigm is irrelevant for the unfolding future. Some people are walking with redundant mindsets that disqualify them for the unfolding dynamics shaping a new paradigm.

Any individual or organisation seeking to perpetuate its existence and relevance should embrace change. An organisation has to beneficially align itself with the environment and should be able to adjust, adapt and create the right linkages that enhance its position within the environment. We cannot muster the new challenges with a mind that is not attuned to the trends and challenges of the times. At the same time we cannot solve problems with the same mind that got us into the respective problem(s). The simple analogy is that we cannot rise from a fall with the same mind that caused us to stagger and fall. Politics has learnt the pitfalls of rigid ideological orientation. It is against that background that most political parties have been adjusting their dosage by moving across the continuum from the left to the right across the centre or vice-versa depending on the dynamics of the political environment in different countries. However, some political establishments are simply redundant and are stuck in traditionalism.

The Fundamentals of Change

The notion of change is as real as life itself. The legendary Peter Drucker will assert that: "change is the only certainty." Any attempt to remain in the past would quicken the end for an organization and all it stands for. To remain contemporary, change is a necessity. Throughout history every paradigm that prevailed necessitated change and adapting or initiating it to survive.

Today's digital acceleration has very little room for the defenders of the status quo. To make a difference we have to harness the challenges and act decisively to win the competitive warfare. The environment will not tune in to your organisation's circumstances. Mary-Anne D. Ponti (2011) would argue that an everyday experience of making something different. She further asserts that change exists on an individual, organizational, and societal level, national, regional and global level change often presents daunting challenges for leaders. Change is inherently disruptive; it creates a sense of uncertainty and fear.

The daunting challenge for change includes the dramatically high failure rate. According to Steigenberger (2015): "Change is an integral part of everyday life. Change creates disturbances and forces people to re-think their current and future situation. To preserve the ability to act in confusing situations, people develop a subjectively plausible story of what meaning, cause and consequence a certain development has and what an appropriate course of action would be. This process of interpreting inputs is widely known as sensemaking (Maitlis, 2005; Weick et al., 2005)." Furthermore it is important to note that: "Inter-personal sensemaking is a story-building process, in which group members may voice their opinion and may try to influence others in order to anchor their individual point of view in the group account produced." (Steigenberger, 2015).

The Change Process

The process of change is not a standard universal sequence of steps that will apply to every situation in the same way. A whole array of circumstances can trigger change, whether gradually or suddenly. As already alluded to change is a persistent and recurrent phenomenon which is with us every moment. Successful companies that last long muster the art of change to remain contemporary in the face of the unfolding environmental forces. Not to change renders the organisation irrelevant to the paradigm of the moment and makes it redundant and subsequently cease to exist. The real time news bulletins on the global developments bring updates on multitudes of changes taking place all the time. Lewin postulates that change is about a process of disturbing the current state (unfreezing), then make adjustments (change) and establish a new order (refreeze the future).

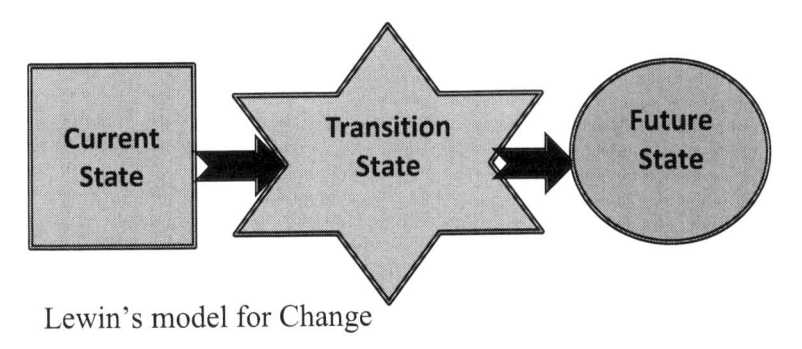

Lewin's model for Change

The Lewin framework provides a simple process that is easy to understand but rather difficult to operationalise. To disturb the current state is not as simple as merely creating disruption, but a complex political process with a lot of resistance because of entrenched positions. The actual innovation to create a new way does not always succeed and that could lead to project failure. The idea of change requires addressing the ethos of the business system and relating that to the expected outcomes of the process of change. The process of change should not be taken in the same context of adopting fashion given that fashion does not necessarily work for everyone. Therefore what is important is to realise the purpose of the respective change and its impact on the bottom line of the organisation's business.

Mega Trends

In 1982 John Nasbitt predicted what he termed mega trends epitomised in the major shifts in the dynamics of the environment. These trends are as follows:

1. Industrial Society to Informational Society: 60% of Americans now work as programmers, teachers, clerks, secretaries, accountants, stock brokers, managers,

insurance people, bureaucrats, lawyers, bankers, technicians, or in healthcare. Manufacturing too now has more information workers.
2. Forced Technology to High-tech/High-touch: the trend away from factory-like production systems to "high" technology robots, computers, and cutting edge automation requires a greater sense of self and closeness with others.
3. National Economy to World Economy: although we're more likely to compare industries between nations, industries are becoming global. Example, automobiles share components made worldwide.
4. Short-term to Long-term: we are becoming more aware of the long term implications of short term fixes and strategies.
5. Centralization to Decentralization: best performing companies increase the autonomy of workers across organizations, at all levels in the hierarchy. Control is maintained through a

nucleus of shared values (common culture).
6. Representative Democracy to Participatory Democracy: People must be a part of the decisions affecting their lives. Employees assert their rights as citizens work
7. Hierarchies to Networking: this trend means a shift away from emphasis on the formal, vertical structure of reporting relationships toward a lateral, diagonal, and bottom-up style of management and interaction.
8. Institutional Help to Self-help: for decades institutions such as government, the medical establishment, and the school system were America's buffers against reality — the need for food, education, and healthcare. We are slowly weaning ourselves from our collective dependence, as we learn to trust ourselves and become more self-reliant.
9. North to South: An irreversible restructuring of America is rooted in 3

other Megatrends: a.) the change from industrial to information, b.) the move from national to global, c.) the reorganization from a central to a decentralized society. In 1980 118M Americans lived in the South and West, and 108M in the North and East. In 1982, 17 House seats went South and 2/3 new jobs were created in the sunbelt. Of 18.4M new jobs created from 1968 to 1978 the North and Midwest got 6.1M and South and West got12.3M. At the same time the North lost jobs from Massachusetts to Minnesota now marred by vacant factories & warehouses.

10. Either/Or to Multiple Option:
Personal choices for postwar America remained limited through much of the 1960s. It was an era of "Leave It to Beaver" and "Father Knows Best," men went to work, and women kept house and raised 2.4 children. Phones were black, bath tubs and refrigerators were white, and checks were green. Ford or GMC;

vanilla or chocolate. Sometimes a 3rd choice was added: strawberry, Chrysler, NBC, ABC, or CBS. Homogenous tastes nurtured by mass markets and mass communication are being liberated by niche markets and decentralization.

The Challenge for Strategy and Change

Strategy as a complex process presents many challenges to an individual or to the organisation. In the context of change management it is important to ensure that there is clarity on what needs to be achieved through the change to be implemented. Naturally change attracts a degree of apprehension as it necessitates unlearning old practices and relearning to fit the new order. That process is often prompted by resistance and could even escalate to a point of sabotaging new initiatives. Given that change is about engaging a new process it would often be characterised by experimentation and mistakes which can be seized upon by the doubters to try and scuttle the plans. The change process could be unsettled by changes taking place in the environment. The allocation of resources in planning for strategies could be complex even in a stable environment but become even more complicated as change sets in.

Chapter 5

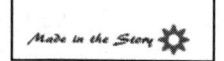

Leadership and Strategy

The three Influence Processes

The definition of management as a process of working with and through others renders itself to a need for mutually cooperating with others within the organisation. Furthermore, organisations ultimately embody teams working at different levels of the management hierarchy. It therefore follows that for leaders to make an impact they should enjoy significant influence to earn the trust and confidence of the followers which in turn submit to their guidance and influence.

There are three main influence processes in management that help create a degree of commitment and respect for the leader. The three influence processes are leadership, motivation and communication. While submissions are made on all the three processes, the main focus will be on leadership given the nature of the topic under consideration.

Communication for Strategy

In simple terms communication is the means by which information is disseminated. Traditionally the written and verbal means of communication have been the main tools. However, the digital era has provided the electronic communication as not only convenience but also prevalent and complex to handle. Anyone can initiate communication via the social networks. While that sounds simple and fast, there is a real danger as the communication could be passed on prematurely or sometimes could be damaging to the organisation.

It is important to acknowledge that information is the bloodstream of the organisation. In that regard to manage business is to manage information. It therefore follows that organisations that can manage information effectively are most likely better managed. Strategic information needs to be gathered and analysed and then determine the timing of when that information can be passed on to the respective people, groups or the whole organisation. We often hear the expression that information is power, indeed it is. However, having information is critical and knowing when and how to disseminate it is equally important. Information should be used to good effect in any give situation, whether to inspire or to deal with a difficult situation there is need for a strategic assessment so that the communication of the respective information or decisions do not give way to harm. The need to manage the communications coming out of an organisation is the main reason why positions like PR manager or head of corporate communications exist. Good leadership would give consideration to who communicates the news, when and where. The basic premise for effective communication is the ability to capture the attention of the audience and present a clear message that does not render itself to misinterpretation.

The best way to communicate is epitomised in simplicity utilising familiar jargon and symbolism. The acronym KISS in communication represents "Keep it simple, stupid." This is necessary as many people are lost in the maze of the technical jargon that ordinary people may struggle with. Information technology and communications (ITC) and the phenomenon of change are the core of the modern day paradigm where everything has become fluid.

Motivation for Strategy

Motivation has received significant attention in management theory as a critical element for getting the best out of people. Given that leadership and strategy is about directing or guiding people towards the realisation of a certain agenda motivation will be a key tenet in getting the desired results. At the heart of motivation is the drive by the leader to galvanize commitment. The leader needs to provide incentives to the team so that they are inspired to perform.

Many theories of motivation have provided, among them Maslow's hierarchy of needs which suggests that needs are ordered rising from basic to higher order needs; Vroom's expectancy theory which underscores that we perform harder and better when the reward is great; Herzberg's two factor theories which underpin motivating and non-motivating factors in an organisation. The idea of what motivates is not something that could be pre-determined as it depends on the people, their culture and the prevailing circumstances of the organisation.

The leader will therefore need to think creatively in order to harness the situation and secure the support of the people being led so that they realise expected results. The big question to ask in motivation is "What makes someone tick and perform".

The Leadership Element in Strategy

Good leaders need to muster a great legacy for their organisation. Great leaders have vision beyond their time in the organisation and are able to cement a robust lasting value system that helps perpetuate the organisation's agenda even when they are gone. Stories of great leaders become an important factor in the socialisation's process for values and culture. In their book *Built to last*, Collins and Porras (1994: p. 2-3) argue the challenge for leadership in pointing out that:

"Visionary companies are premier institutions- the crown jewels in their industries, widely admired by their peers and having a long track record of making significant impact on the world around them. ...All individual leaders, no matter how charismatic or visionary, eventually die; and all visionary products and services- all "great ideas"-eventually become obsolete and disappear. Yet visionary companies prosper over long periods of time, through multiple product life cycles and multiple generations of active leaders."

In trying to understand the facets of a good leader there are a number of words that are common in drawing up the characteristics of a leader. The list may not be exhaustive but it gives an in-depth insight of the notion of leadership.

What is crucial is to understand the fundamentals articulated by Martin Luther King, Jr argued that: "The ultimate measure of a man is not where he stands in moments of comfort and convenience, but where he stands at times of challenge and controversy". Leadership is not about the easy situations but also about dealing with challenging difficult circumstances.

Factors for Leadership

Vision	Values
Courage	Inspiration
Passion	Decisiveness
Single-minded	Informed
Spiritually drilled	Open minded
Well read	Aligned
Good Listener	Assertive
Performer	Negotiator
Likeable	Good image
Inspirational	Great thinker
Selling Instinct	Calculating
Focus	Goal driven
Entrepreneurial/	Intrapreneurial
Efficient/Effective	Charismatic
Communicator	Motivational

The Globe leadership research survey identifies a number of positive attributes for leaders. The positive traits of leadership include the following:

Trustworthy	Honest
Encouraging	Positive
Dynamic	Motivator
Dependable	Intelligent
Decisive	Communicative
Informed	Team builder
Win-win problem-solver	Plans ahead

On the contrary there are also negative traits that characterise some leaders. The respective traits are listed below.

Loner	Asocial	Irritable
Dictatorial	Ruthless	Non-cooperative
Egocentric		

The practice of leadership necessitates having certain skills for handling situations in

organisations. Bejoy Matthew puts forward the 5 D's that a leader needs as summarised below:
1. Discover, 2. Drive, 3. Delegate, 4. Delay, 5. Delete. The essence of the 5 D's is that a leader should see through situations and discover or uncover new ways. If results are to be realised the leader would need to galvanize energies for performance. A leader should also assign others to take responsibility for the performance of tasks. Leaders should calculate implications of any activity and avoid rushed action or decision. As a leader one should not hold onto issues or ideas that are no longer relevant or more appropriately expire hence they need to remove the unnecessary baggage. In the same context Prof Sattar Bawany who is the CEO & C-Suite Master Executive Coach of Centre for Executive Education (CEE Global) advances emotional & social intelligence competencies of highly effective leaders. The factors attributed to the phenomenon of leadership are:

1. Self-Awareness, 2. Assertiveness, 3. Empathy, 4. Independence, 5. Communication,

6. Feedback. The factors identified are simple to comprehend but go deeper into the ethos of leadership. A good leader would know his/her strengths and weaknesses and play accordingly. A good leader needs to be firm when decided on something instead of being rather inconsistent, thus sending mixed signals. Good leaders would put themselves in the shoes of other people as they decide or when they face challenges. Effective leaders are able to stand on their own ground and not be swayed easily. Effective leaders are good communicators and people rally behind them. Good leaders provide those who follow them with appropriate information about how things transpire in order to keep them informed, address short comings or acknowledge their good performance. Adam and Adams (2000: p. 15) advance the critical importance of transformational leadership in arguing that: "Transformational leaders respond adaptively to situations and see risk-taking as a necessity, and opportunity for innovation and problem-solving. Such leadership is inclusive; it articulates a shared vision for the future and encourages those

involved to feel that they're a part of something bigger, and to have a hand in defining what "bigger" will mean. ... Beyond sharing a vision for change, they develop the role of leadership throughout the organization, creating an expanded group of leaders."

Lessons for Leadership

Rich Conlow presents important lessons for leadership from the experiences and practices of great leaders from the past. While the different lessons are attributed to individuals, that does make them mutually exclusive.

Nelson Mandela, having spent 27 years in prison became president of South Africa.
Lesson 1 is to be clear on your values.

Lucius Quinctius Cincinnatus became leader in Italy having been persecuted and relinquished power in weeks.
Lesson 2 reminds us to lead with integrity.

Dr. Martin Luther King inspired the Afro-Americans a civil rights leader who was assassinated but left a legacy in whose call Obama the first Afro-American president is born.

Lesson 3: the greatest leaders have a vision or dream that inspires others to follow them.

George Washington was the first president of the United States of America who worked well and served only for two terms and set the precedent for modern day American democracy.

Lesson 4: a leader's role is to serve.

Alexander the Great built a great empire conquering nations and integrating cultures. He established himself as the man who conquered the world.

Lesson 5 is that passion drives success.

Ashoka the Great is an Indian leader who ruled the Asian subcontinent and after many deaths in building his empire he retired. He then went on to live a selfless life as a patron of Buddha.

Lesson 6 is that great leaders learn, grow and change.

Abraham Lincoln is a man of perseverance who faced setbacks but still remained resolute in pursuing his goal. He loved peace and tranquility and championed the great civil war. He is credited with the emancipation act that freed slaves.

Lesson 7 is that to lead effectively you have to communicate, influence and persuade positively.

Mahatma Gandhi was educated in South Africa and practised law. He returned to India where he organised people to free India from British rule without firing a gun.

Lesson 8 is that great leaders enable others to act by unifying them into cooperative and effective work groups or teams.

Mother Theresa was born in Albania, worked in Ireland before moving to India to live and work with the poor and revolutionised their lives. She has a huge following.

Lesson 9 is lead by example.

Julius Caesar was a mighty military leader and politician who championed the great Roman empire. He thoroughly trained his troops.

Lesson 10 is that if you train your people the best, they will perform the best.

The Biblical Lessons on Leadership

The greatest strategist is God for all creation, the past, the present and the future, everything visible and everything invisible is his plan. The unfolding issues in the bible demonstrate a great masterplan that embraces all things and all situations in leadership. According to Lorin Woolfe the main biblical lessons on leadership embrace the following issues:

- Honesty and integrity
- Purpose
- Kindness and compassion
- Humility

- Communication
- Performance management
- Team development
- Courage
- Justice and fairness
- Leadership development

Throughout the bible from the Old Testament to the New Testament these qualities are vivid. When Adam acted without integrity he lost the favour of God. In today's world when people act without integrity they lose credibility and the support of the followers. King David the most successful king of Israel had courage, was purpose-driven and was a good communicator. Jesus Christ represents the ultimate example in serving God and living an exemplary life on earth. He is principle centred, humble, accommodating and above all guided by well-founded values and principles of the kingdom. Complementary to the work of Jesus Christ, the son of God the main architect in setting the foundation for Christianity as a global phenomenon was Paul the man who was converted from persecuting the church of Jesus.

Paul sold the idea of Christianity to Romans, Jews and other gentiles with passion through power selling and networking. It is clear that St Paul's approach is well founded in that he was a visionary who acted relentlessly on his dream and the ideals he worked have spanned generations well after he is long gone. He is someone termed a "power seller"- somebody selling on a wider scope, with speed and passion. Robert Burke (2006) advances the case for leadership and spirituality suggesting that a higher purpose of life beyond materialism will lead to more effective leadership and better performance.

Chapter 6

Made in the Story

The Strategic Mindset of the Eagle

Introduction

The eagle has positive connotations attributed to it in respect of its character in most cultures. The eagle is a bird of prey which swoops and grabs its prey with speed. It scales the heights rendering its prey weak before feasting on it. The eagle is crafty, swift, focused and is like a laser guided missile in its ability to see from a high altitude and strike accurately. The eagle would descent from a high altitude like a rocket, swooping on an unsuspecting target, and in a split second it will be scaling the heights holding onto its prey and shocking it into submission and confusion.

Engel (2007: p. 44) in an article on *The Soaring Eagle: The Power of Resilience,* would state that: "The eagle represents strength, vision, and endurance; unaffected by the storms, it soars above. How is it that some children bounce back from adversity and persevere through difficult times? In one word: resiliency." Resilience underpins a struggle to thrive against adversity and excel. That calls on one to champion a revolution on a personal level; it is about defying the circumstances to reach out for something even better.

In the logic of Margret Wheatley, this is *walking out and walking on*, ie., get out of something retrogressive or limiting and move to something progressive. Wolin and Wolin (1993) quoted in Engel (2007: 47) provide seven attributes of resistance for child treatment in soaring above adversity as: "insight, independence, relationships, initiative, humour, creativity, and morality, the most powerful of the seven... Resilient survivors are perceptive, teachable, savvy, and deliberate in their choices and choose to build strong, healthy families." While Engel puts forward these key arguments in respect of child behaviour the logic is applicable to every facet of life where human endeavour is required to make a difference. Without daring to overcome adversity there would be no human advancement. It would follow that to progress and advance humanity, risks have to be taken. In the process results unfold; whether good or bad. Irrespective of the result there is always the next step; either we celebrate, reflect, learn and take the next step.

Resilience and Advance in the Kingdom

While thinking and reflecting on the ethos of the characteristics of the eagle I note the prevalence of the same approach in the bible. A typical reference to the soaring power of the eagle is provided in Isaiah 40: 31: "But they that wait upon the Lord shall renew their strength; they shall mount up with wings as eagles; they shall run, and not be weary; and they shall walk, and not faint." This scripture resonates with the idea of soaring and being resilient. In the case of Jesus resilience is expressed in the scripture, Luke 13: 31-32: "The same day there came certain of the Pharisees, saying unto him, Get thee out, and depart hence: for Herod will kill thee. And he said unto them, Go ye, and tell that fox, behold, I cast out devils, and I do cures today and tomorrow, and the third day I shall be perfected."

Jesus would not be detracted from his mission because of the threats from Herod. Furthermore, it is a biblical truism that Christ appeared on earth on a mission to destroy the agenda of the evil one: "He that committeth sin is of the devil; for the devil sinneth from the beginning. For this purpose the Son of God was manifested, that he might destroy the works of the devil." In terms of the strategic thought process the devil is the evil one who should be outwitted and destroyed.

Surprise Strike and Battle Ground Control

An eagle enjoys rising high into space reaching altitudes of 10000 to 15000 feet. They can see their prey from such heights and descend to attack at speeds of 200 mph (miles per or hour) or 320 km/h (kilometres per hour). The eagle's ability to move from high altitudes like a bullet comes with an element of surprise which shocks the prey which is attacked off guard. The eagle has powerful wings and its claws have a strong grip that ensures that it does not lose its prey while scaling the heights.

A good example is when an eagle attacks a snake. Snakes are poisonous, dangerous and alert to the enemy attack. However, an eagle shocks the snake through surprise; further confuses it with speed carrying it into space. Once the eagle carrying the snake reaches a certain height it becomes powerless, vomits the poison and becomes a ready meal for the eagle. Therefore the eagle gains control of the situation firstly through surprise and secondly through changing the battleground. If the eagle was to remain on the ground chances for victory are reduced. The poisonous snake can easily strike the eagle on the ground and kill it, but cannot do the same in space. The versatility of the eagle provides an advantage as it enables it to change the tactics for fighting. Put another way, an eagle will play to its strength in space or on the land. The eagle changes the battle space and rules of the fight in its favour by scaling the heights.

Scaling the Heights and Adaptation

The eagle scales the heights surveying the space below looking for prey. At the same time the eagle allows the environment to elevate it. The eagle can ride on a storm and scale the heights. That means an eagle can adapt to difficult situations with easy by letting the storm carry it. In real life or business circumstances many people collapse under a storm while others adapt to circumstances and thrive. It is important to note that we cannot prosper when we give in to a storm and surrender. We should understand that every crisis is a passing phase as no situation lasts forever. There are many people who have faced terrible afflictions in their lives and managed to turnaround their situations and ended up celebrating major breakthroughs in their lives. Every person has an opportunity to make a difference in life irrespective of the storms they have faced or thorns that have pierced them. One can recover from any situation and excel just like the eagle can ride a storm and continue in its life.

Chapter 7

Made in the Story

The Strategic Mind of the Crocodile

The universal approach in fighting

The crocodile presents a robust universal approach to fighting. The crocodile is a reptile that enjoys living on land and in water. The crocodile has a thick skin with shells whose skin is not easily hurt. The scales especially on the tail form a strong weapon which it uses in attacking its prey. The crocodile has the flexibility to effectively engage in a fight on the land and in water.

The approach of the crocodile is a key factor in corporate competitiveness and adaptation. Just like a crocodile will fight on land and in water a fit organisation will adapt to different business environments locally and internationally where there is increased diversity. In international marketing the notion of adaptation is a key factor in exploiting markets and it is even more imperative when an organisation goes global like Coca-Cola. Many organisations have had to learn fast the art of adaptation in order to sustain business in the diverse set of markets it faces on the global front.

The Fighting Approach

As already alluded to the crocodile is a universal fighter with a powerful approach in every sphere of battle. The crocodile will give a robust fight, unhindered by the environment, whether in the water or on the land. If attacked from the front or if it goes for its prey from the front it will bite. When the crocodile bites it releases some poison but more importantly, it tears the prey with its sharp teeth. At the same time its bite is like a vice grip as it is not easily shaken off the prey. That means even if the opposition tries to shake off to be freed it is certain to be torn from the bite. Often this is not a simple but rather a deep wound that hurts and weakens the prey or the opposition. This bite is like a killer punch in a boxing ring where the opponent is knocked out (KO). This is the challenge for effective business where the strategic moves should knock out the competition. Good business is anchored on winning against competition and to win one would need to outdo the opposition with a strong punch or bite in this case. Therefore on the land crocodile will employ power and the sharp bite to overpower the prey or attacker.

When the battle shifts into water the game takes a more robust approach. While still employing the powerful grip in the bite the crocodile's tail becomes a decisive tool for attack. The tail can flash water at the unsuspecting prey. Either the prey is grabbed by the mouth or is firstly slashed with the tail almost like being struck by a sword. Immediately the crocodile will then grab the prey with its mouth. The tail creates a hook that holds water so that the prey cannot drag the crocodile out of the water. At this point the crocodile operates like a four wheel drive car that pulls from both the front and the back and can manoeuvre its way in the most rough terrain.

It is important to note that the crocodile's approach is versatile and adaptive to the terrain and the situation of the prey. The idea of adaptation in business is often brought up in international business where an organisation has to embrace different cultures. A crocodile does not suffocate because of the change of the environment; instead it finds the best way to fight. Organisations and individuals should be flexible in approach and be prepared to adjust and embrace the changes to the business circumstances. Resistance to change is an acknowledgement that human beings struggle to adapt to a new model of business.

From the characteristics of the crocodile's approach to fighting it is clear that a number of terms capture the ethos of the crocodile mentality and they include; adaptability, strength of punch, impact on prey, surprise in attack, criticality of timing and disguise in attack. By employing the above mentioned characteristics the crocodile wins as hunter hunt for prey and a fighter.

Summary of the Crocodile Mentality

The crocodile emerges as a universal fighter with a powerful grip. The crocodile can still earn a meal while relaxed with its mouth open. The reptile will use its powerful bite to tear into the body of its prey. In water the crocodile will move with its body immersed under water and only its nose just above the surface of the water. That could be difficult to identify for the prey. That in essence presents the crocodile with an element of surprise as it attacks prey which might be unsuspecting. It could attack with either of two approaches. The crocodile could splash water and strike the prey with its tail. Alternatively the crocodile could simply grab the mouth of the prey drinking water and drag it into the water. From the approach of the crocodile it is clear this versatile approach makes it a winner on the land and in water. That characteristic implies that as individuals or organisations there is need for versatility in dealing with the environment. We need to understand how to play the game in different contexts or need to be adaptable to the turf on which the battle is fought.

Chapter 8

The Strategic Mind of the Snake

The Enemy of Man

A snake is a creature of hate for man. The biblical story puts the snake at the heart of human disobedience to God for influencing man to disobey God. Snakes are ordinarily seen as a symbol of evil and therefore any time people come across snakes the interpretation is often that it is a bad omen in most cultures. In Genesis 3: 1 the bible says that: "Now the serpent was more crafty than any beast of the field which the Lord God had made." So while the snake is considered evil the bible acknowledges that it was the wisest of all animals. In Matthew 10: 16 the bible says that: ""I am sending you out like sheep among wolves. Therefore be as shrewd as snakes and as innocent as doves." Once more the snake is acknowledged as wise.

Therefore the snake has wisdom that even man is urged to observe. Therefore, it follows that by observing the snake's characteristics we could derive some wisdom. As much as snakes are hated, there is a lot to learn from them; even more importantly from this book we can discern a lot of logical thinking in the context of strategy. A lot of the qualities of the snake are drawn from the bible where the snake depicts both evil and wisdom. The snake has some unique qualities that make it peculiar despite the connotations snakes attract from people.

The Snake is Focused

The snake has a sharp eye and is quick to raise its head when it senses danger. This is a big challenge to individuals and businesses. There is a tendency for organisations to walk blindly into problems. We are often unconcerned about what would be happening in the environment until we start experiencing problems. We have a tendency to wait for a crisis before we could act. This shortcoming is prevalent at individual, corporate and national levels. The various disparities in competitive, adoption of technologies and overall economic development are largely due to blind walking in the terrain of life and business. Snakes are on the watch out for possible attacks; and that gives snakes an edge over the ordinary person's approach.

Snakes rarely move in groups ensuring that there is focus one one's business. Whenever there are too many players commotion often follows unless there is someone to manage the situation. The common English says that: "Too many cooks spoil the broth". We could therefore say that a snake minds its own business. Many times we fail to stand out because we are busy looking at others and comparing ourselves. The snake meanwhile will be busy focused on its mission and not worry about anybody's success or failure. A snake does not have a sense of hearing but senses through vibrations. This could mean that a snake does not have time for gossip which humans seem to suffer from. We dwell too much on what will be happening which is not important, forgetting the core business. The sensing and alertness of a snake can point to the need for environmental awareness in strategic thinking.

Strategic Attacker and Killer

Snakes are ruthless attackers. Snakes can strike and kill in an instant sometimes when the victim is not even aware that they are coming under attack. Some snakes could be so docile that the unsuspecting victim could step onto them and they are struck. Many snakes are lethal in their attack causing instant death or without the necessary injection the victim could be dead in a short time. The snake has venom or poison which makes its strike very dangerous. That strike from the snake if likened to business could be termed a category killer, that is a move that paralyses a business system. The introduction of laptops meant desktops increasingly lost their appeal and now tablets and ipads are making laptops increasingly less fashionable. Ebay has made conventional auctioning for personal items less appealing. These kinds of punches are similar to the snake bite which simply immobilizes the enemy who might die. The organisation needs a killer instinct in its operations.

Strategic Momentum

Snakes do not make noise when they move as they do not have legs. The glide on their belly and can be so fast. As they move they are not likely to attract the attention of the enemy; they can always surprise the enemy.

Chapter 9

The Complete Strategic Mindset

Understanding Completeness

The Collins English dictionary defines complete as *adj. 1. Thorough; absolute: it was a complete shambles. 2. Perfect in quality or in kind: he is the complete modern footballer. 3. Finished. 4. Having all the necessary parts. 5. Complete with as an extra feature or part; mansion complete with a swimming pool. 6. To finish. 7. To make whole or perfect.* To be omplete borders on being fully facilitated or having a perfect approach which is a tall order to attain. Given the complexity of strategy it is a big challenge to have a complete strategic mindset. The big challenge is that with the terrain of business or life shifting according to the paradigm of the moment the complete or perfect player must be adaptable and incorporate the challenges of the times.

In a ground breaking conceptual approach to strategic posturing the Miles and Snow typology presents a continuum of orientations across a range of levels of engagement. These levels include a reactor, defender, analyser and prospector. Each orientation suggests a different approach or mindset in handling the moves an ndividual or organisation makes. The prospector seeks change and would initiate it. The analyser is cautious in embracing change. The defender would try and maintain the status quo and would resist change. The reactor is unprepared and will only change as a response to a crisis.

These different levels or postures are positional, cognitive and perceptual and therefore demand that strategists should be versatile as every organisation at some point may need to embrace one position or another of these orientations as the environment dictates. Vestal would assert that: "Having a strategic mindset implies new ways to create solutions and a dynamic plan by which patient, staff, business, and professional issues can converge. Such strategies lead to a plan from which action steps can be developed and executed." Therefore, strategic thinking and formulation leads to a new posture and its dynamics to reposition the organisation and charter a way forward. While determining the future moves is essential, that process should be in tandem with the trends of the environment. Jim Haudan (2000) writing in the Leadership Excellence magazine suggests that there are four key issues that underpin successful management for strategies in an organistation, which are:

1. Know the business;
2. Know their role;
3. Know how to connect their teams to the business; and
4. Know how to deliver results through their teams.

These submissions underpin the call for excellence in executing strategy. A business model designed and operationalised should be a winner in the market with teams guided to get the results and grow the business. The ultimate call for every business or management engagement demands efficiency and effectiveness (optimal cost performance and getting results).

The Strategic Challenges

In an article on strategic marketing Brownie (1998) quotes (Locke, 1961, p. 248) ". . . the faculty which God has given man to supply the want of clear and certain knowledge in cases where it cannot be had, . . . is judgement..." Therefre, whatever challenge individuals or organisations face where the situation is vague they need to make a judgement on how to deal with it. In strategy it is common that we have to deal with grey areas and therefore it is mandatory that the development of strategies is associated with judgement. It is important to note that today was shaped in yesterday's judgements in dealing with the uncertainties faced in the past.

Strategy is a complex process that requires an understanding of the past, the present and the future. The past takes organisations to the present, which in turn ushers in the future. While we manage for the future, it is critical to note that the future can be as easy or as difficult as the present shapes it. Preparation for the future in the present makes it easier to handle it as it unfolds. Strategy is like a road map. A city built without projecting future growth would be very difficult to manage with narrow roads failing to cope with population growth and the sewer system bursting. To the contrary a city that gives scope for growth will readily accommodate expansion and makes it easier to handle the numbers. An effective strategic planning process can save an organisation a lot of costs associated with failing to plan. The old adage holds that "Failing to plan is planning to fail." A realistic plan helps avert failure in personal life or in business.

Besides having the foresight to think in a futuristic manner connected to the present an organisation has to embrace change by beneficially aligning itself with the dynamic environment. Put another way, a strategic mindset needs to adjust the business model in tandem with the paradigm of the moment and should mirror the paradigm shift as times change. Most businesses had to learn fast and tune into the dictates of a globalised business world in the 1990s and at the turn of the century. Everyone's expectation today is to do business online and that is it; irrespective of the feelings of the organisation and its leaders that order has to to be embraced if the organisation is to perpetuate its existence and relevance.

A strategic approach necessitates learning on the part of the organisation. This challenge sounds rather ironic; given that on one end an organisation needs to be innovative but at the same time the organisation would need to develop a standard and adapt to the environment. One other aspect of strategic thinking that remains very critical is the development of systems and structures that facilitate the realisation of the chosen strategy.

A strategic mindset demands a winning mentality. Oftentimes business is about fighting for markets against competition, whether direct or indirect competition. The competitive game requires differential positioning or some element of dominance which helps win against the other players in the business environment. Michael Porter, the Harvard professor provides simple, but effective frameworks for understanding competition and how to compete in the market. First he provides the five forces as the drivers of competition which include the bargaining power of buyers; the bargaining power of suppliers; the rivalry amongst current players in the market; availability of substitutes and potential entrants into the market. The play of these forces will shape the intensity of the competition. Michael Porter's dosage on how to compete is epitomised in three strategies; which are a focus or niching approach; cost leadership and differentiation.

While these three approaches clearly guide an organisation to successful performance, Porter berets the company without a clear strategy as stuck in the middle, virtually confused or mixed up as a poor performer without direction.

In 1964 Ted Levitt one of the marketing gurus put forward a powerful argument which has proven prophetic. He argued about the global village becoming a reality. His assertion was that as the convergence of needs and easy transportation and communicatin would lead to the realisation of a true global market where everyone will have access to services and products from across the globe. This era has not only made this a reality but instead has become a way of life by placing the globe in one's palm in the power of the mobile phone with the cost of communication becoming next to zero with many free web based applications making it free to communicate globally. At the same time many real time instant broadcasting options by multiple players have made virtual experience a global experience for great events or breaking news a commonality.

The ongoing global story is within reach with news updated constantly institutionally and by individuals through social networks. People power has been compounded through readily available information, multiplicity of channels and enhanced mass communication. Some dictators were removed from power through the power of social media; and an African American, Barrack Obama made it to the Whitehouse through the aid of the power of the social media in 2008 and in 2012. While the availability of information makes it easy to inform and gain understanding it can also make it very difficult to decide because of information overkill, too much information becoming difficult to discern and make sense. This demands decisiveness on the part of managers.

The nature of work and the machinery and equipment used is sophisticated. As a result the training required to handle such complex machinery is advanced. Therefore, human resources management demands an advanced approach to be able to harness the modern challenges in the paradigm of the moment. Most employees require some information technology training to be functional in an organisation. Most of the operations are computerised hence, making the assertion by Adam Smith in 1789 prophetic. He argued the significance of the 3Ss which represent *simplification, standardisation* and *specialisation.* These processes have become even more important in this generation and would shape successful organisations going forward. The notion of simplification relates to the easy with which certain processes can be executed. Simpler systems are easy to manage. Standardisation has become a defining factor in competitiveness across national boundaries with systems like the ISO 9000 being catalysts opening windows for international markets. Specialisation provides the focus to perfect the art of doing something which leads to excellence in execution. Through specialisation individuals and organisations realise outstanding results and advance the quality of life an experience of consuming the respective goods and services.

Towards a Successful Complete Strategic Mindset

The real call to strategize demands strength and fearlessness in facing the challenges of a dynamic environment. Margret Wheatley (2008: pp.14-15) a leadership expert asserts that: "...Pressures on leaders have increased dramatically. They no longer have time or flexibility. They feel caged, oppressed, exhausted." Therefore, in facing up to the challenges of a complete strategic mindset one has to think far and wide without losing focus on what really matters. In considering the diversity of challenges faced by an organisation the complete strategic mindset will necessity the qualities epitomised in the thought processes and orientation of the crocodile, the eagle and the snake. In the first instance the general mindset should be tuned to success. John Leach (2010) provides a number of elements that underscore the success factor shaping a success mindset; and they include the following factors:

- Vision
- Passion "Nothing great in the world has been accomplished without passion" George Wilhelm Friedrich Hegel. "If I had to name a driving force in my life, I would name passion every time." Anita Roddick
- Smart Goals/objectives
- Sense of purpose
- Shared vision
- Align- head, heart wallet
- Define values – "If we are to go forward, we must go back and rediscover those precious values – that all reality hinges on moral foundations and that all reality has a spiritual control." Martin Luther King, Jr
- Change your Mindset: "To create something exceptional your mindset must be relentlessly focused on the smaller detail."

- Grasp the opportunities: Life's race well run, life's work well done." Grave inscription, anonymous
- Vision without action is hallucination
- Build resolve: "If you are going through hell, keep going."
- Reflect and Recharge
- Deal with loneliness-Be hopeful beyond hope.
- Connect to the community- "Shared joy is double joy; shared sorrow is half a sorrow."
- Tap into mindsets
- Reinforce key messages
- Earn respect
- Build a personal brand
- Be consistent
- Unleash your enthusiasm
- Relationships
- Gain an edge
- Creative thinking
- Challenge your conventional wisdom
- Bring your ideas to life
- Be decisive

- Embrace pressure
- Gain momentum fast
- Be confident

The Framework for the Complete Strategic Mindset

Kinichi Ohmae the Japanese strategist provides the 3C's at the centre of the strategy process. These elements include company, customer and competition. This perspective has both an internal and external perspective of the strategy process. Pellegrino and Carbo (2001: p. 375) argue that: "When strategy is deep and far reaching, then what you gain in your calculation is much, so you can win even before you fight. When your strategic thinking is shallow and nearsighted, then what you gain by your calculations is little, so you lose before you do battle." In the thinking and frame of thinking of this book the complete strategic mindset is epitomised in the orientations or approaches of the crocodile, the eagle and the snake.

In short the crocodile is a strong complete fighter from every angle or platform; from the front or from the back, in the water or on the land. The eagle scales the heights, moves with speed and surprises targets. The snake is single minded and slick mover with a strong sense of security and always watching over the enemy moves. The challenge for appropriate, accurate and swift decision-making is even more critical in the light of globalisation and fast changing technology. This has led Woiceshyn (2009) to argue that: "To understand the ability to make such decisions, much research and the popular business press have focused on the role of intuition, defined as "insight that bypasses reasoning" and commonly understood as an inexplicable "hunch" or "gut feeling" that tells a person what to do." The case for using intuition in coming up with outstanding decisions is significant as it accounts for the between good and bad performers. Woiceshyn (2009) points out that most decision makers combine intuition and rational decision-making. Woiceshyn goes on to point out that good minds for decision making are guided by integrated essentials while bad minds are not. Ultimately Woiceshyn (2009) provided the factors that characterise the good mind or the effective CEO as:

- Look for essentials

- Identify and apply principles

- Spiral to refine your decision

- Focus your mind on facts

- Introspect

- Find and follow your passion

In a study on entrepreneurship Barbara Sahakian, a professor of neuro-psychology at Cambridge University, assembled two groups of business people in their early 50s. She identified important characteristics that resonate with good leadership as follows:

Resilience: Focus that is unshaken in good and bad times.
Interdependence: Mutual cooperation and cross-pollination on doing tasks.

Networking skills: Ability to connect and build relationships.

Learn to sell: Developing skills on how to sell.
Strap yourself in – it's a bumpy ride: Remaining positive even when mist or confusion sets in.

Action orientation: Be focused on getting things done.

Perseverance: Hold on against delays or adversity in trying to realise the objectives.

Thirst for knowledge: Be a knowledge seeker so that there are no gaps that cannot be understood.

Sacrifice: Some trade-offs have to be accepted if something great is to be achieved. There may be need to forego certain benefits in order to realise the objective.

Arguing the case for modern day strategy Josh Bernoff (2014) points the mobile mind of the modern times: "The Mobile Mind Shift, successful companies follow four steps represented by the acronym IDEA: identify, design, engineer and analyze. ...Mobile moments are the new locus of competition. Be there in your customer's mobile moment and you gain their loyalty." The speed of processing and convenience for the customer is paramount; the digital error has removed patience from service delivery phenomenon and payment. Everyone is looking for instant performance and payment. The mobile technology is now connecting everyone to servers facilitating business exchanges.

The Framework for the Complete Strategic Mindset

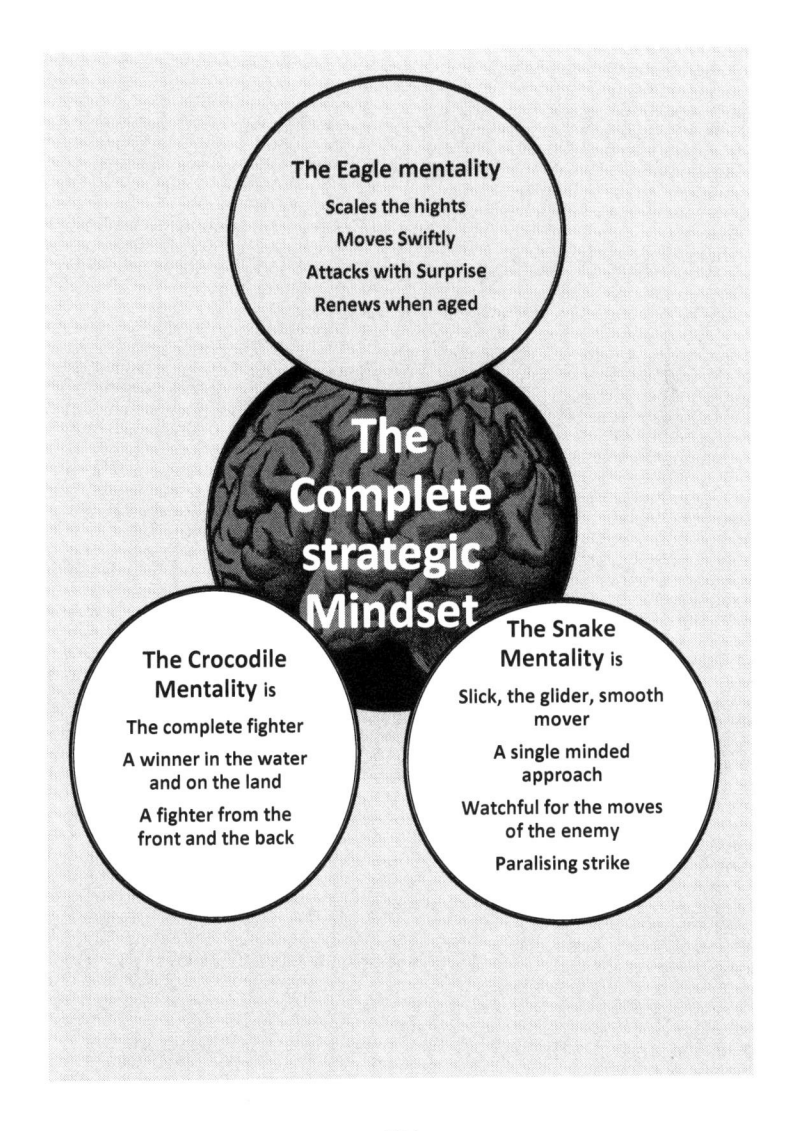

The Eagle mentality
Scales the hights
Moves Swiftly
Attacks with Surprise
Renews when aged

The Complete strategic Mindset

The Crocodile Mentality is
The complete fighter
A winner in the water and on the land
A fighter from the front and the back

The Snake Mentality is
Slick, the glider, smooth mover
A single minded approach
Watchful for the moves of the enemy
Paralising strike

Lessons from Steve Jobs

Steve Jobs is one of the most iconic figures in recent years. His life speaks volumes through his ingenuity as an entrepreneur and inventor at Apple. His vision of championing voice and motion has transformed humanity to the point of making technology the toy for all age groups. We are glued on short videos and messaging that has spread from the Apple initiatives to other technological companies. The brand apple speaks volumes as a provider of value. While Jobs sadly passed away his legacy remains a hallmark of success at Apple. Carmine Gallo, the author of *The Presentation Secrets of Steve Jobs* and *The Innovation Secrets of Steve Jobs*, provides the principles for success with the product or the brand for Steve Jobs. The seven principles identified can be employed by anyone to succeed are as follows:

Principle One: ***Do what you love***. Steve Jobs did what he loved, the idea of excellence with technology. He would say to some employess that "People with passion can change the world for the better." Carmine Gallo would point that Steve followed his passion throughout his life. What this means is that if one has a passion they must be relentless in seeking to perfect and excel in it. Mediocrity cannot lead to stardom. You will appreciate how much the sporting champions sweat in practice to perfect their art.

Principle Two: *Put a dent in the universe*. Carmine Galo would say that: "Passion fuels the rocket, but vision directs the rocket to its ultimate destination." Whatever, idea people have and have a burning desire to excel in, it means nothing without the foresight of its long term impact to the marketplace. Visionary people are imaginative and creative in shaping the future. This is the notion of competing for the future, the idea that was made popular by the Harvard professors, Gary Hamel and Prahalad in the 1990s. If anyone had an idea to make a difference it demands that they perceive a future world in which their idea will shape humanity in some way. Steve Jobs saw everyone with a computer, and certainly to this day that is the reality.

Principle Three: **Kick start your brain**. Carmine Galo quotes Steve Jobs as saying "Creativity is connecting things." Great ideas do not necessarily have to be without precedence. The idea of copy and improve is at the heart of innovation. Many of the inventions that we see today have their roots in something observed, whether through observing nature or other industries and professions. If you want to excel it is mandatory to have open eyes and ears then reflect and imagine.

Principle Four: **Sell dreams, not products**. To Steve Jobs believed in creating inspiration in the buyer of products. He perceived them as having hopes, dreams, ambitions and aspirations. If the promise made to a customer did not bring an imagination to see an exciting world they might not be motivated.

Principle Five: *Say no to 1,000 things*. Steve Jobs believed in simplicity in the technology that would encourage the users to acquire the technology. This principle concurs Adam Smith's notion of simplification as a key element of effective manufacturing.

Principle Six: *Create insanely great experiences*.

Apple stores are modelled on the principle of creating great experiences. The stores are manned by experts and not mere cashiers. That allows for creative people to help shape the best experiences for the customers. Steve Jobs said that: "Be a yardstick of quality. Some people aren't used to an environment where excellence is expected." In concurrence with that assertion Oprah Winfrey would say that: "Surround yourself with people who will take you higher."

Principle Seven: *Master the message*. Carmine Galo describes Steve Jobs as: "the world's greatest corporate storyteller, turning product launches into an art form." It is imperative that whatever we do there is no way we could make a difference without telling an inspiring story. Everything worth noting is a story. Our whole being is part of a web of stories and therefore it is imperative to harness the art of storytelling and use it to make great brands. I am the author of the book, *Story it! Brand it! Sell it!* and I am persuaded that storytelling is key to human understanding and motivation having done my PhD on story branding.

Chapter 10

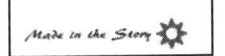

Made in the Story ✸

Stop Dreaming! Act Now

Results come from Action

No amount of thinking and meditating alone will move a feather or let alone wipe the dust off a surface. Even with the best of information and experts making a contribution to crafting a strategy that means nothing without action. There is a common saying that says that a journey of a thousand miles starts with one step. A first class planning effort does not automatically render itself to a first class implementation process.

Action is symptomatic of movement. When a strategy has been formulated it needs to be acted upon or executed in a robust manner and that is where the strategic mindset counts. The greatest strategist of all time remains a mystery to most people. For those of faith the underpinning laws of nature, understood or misunderstood resonate with God's predestination. At the heart of all things natural or man-made is the hand of God. The biblical nature of God is epitomised in the first book of the bible in showing God moving over the waters and then speaking creation into existence.

Subsequently man is then created in the image of God. Going by the biblical origin of man it follows that man sees the future before its time, man thinks, man creates, man acts and above all man has authority over all creation. The bible speaks about man's dominion about the earth but man has gone into several other planets and continues to discover. The understanding of mankind of man as God's creation puts man in the best frame of the complete strategic thinking. If we explore the biblical story more we realise how we deal with the enemy, flush them out like lightning. At the same time when one plan fails one engages a turnaround strategy for restoration and that is the manifestation and demonstration of Kingdom power by Jesus Christ, the God man.

The eagle thought process will scale the heights and can see from a long distance. At the same time the action of an eagle is decisive and swift. Well thought out strategies require calculated swift and decisive action in order to meet the objectives set out. There has to be an element of surprise if strategy is to be effective because the idea is to outwit the competition by striking unexpectedly. An eagle's approach is visionary in that it sees afar and determines the action to hit the target with speed and power. Even more importantly the eagle has a sensor for redundancy emanating from old age and essentially will not just die. The eagle has a perennial mentality that allows it to go through a rigorous process to rejuvenate and renew itself.

Some individuals and organisations appear to suffer from inertia and tend to give in very quickly. They fail to act decisively cannot renew themselves to remain contemporary. What is needed is visionary thinking which enables an organisation to project future strategic positions and rally the troops towards a watershed.

While the use of the term vision is commonly used in ordinary talk, it appears many people do not see beyond their noses; most people have the here and now kind of mentality. Organisations like Apple, Virgin, Econet, Alibaba, BMW, Tesco, Toyota among others are visionary, hence they have staying power in a challenging business environment. The idea is to see a future position and prepare for it before getting there. Visionary organisations do not merely adapt but also contribute to the shaping of the environment.

The mind of the snake complements the mind of the eagle in the realisation of a strategy. Snakes do not hear with ears but sense through vibration and that reduces the disturbances that snakes experience. Oftentimes when a creature has a sense of hearing every sound causes some disturbance to it and that does not apply to snakes. Snakes concentrate on what really matters, ie., movement by the enemy instead of every sound that may not necessarily matter. Put another way snakes are not affected by every wave like gossipers who will stop what matters to attend to what is irrelevant.

It is not common for snakes to move in groups or pairs, and that suggests that snakes are single minded. Many people or organisations tend to have divided opinions and are mixed up on whether to go forward or backwards. Snakes do not preoccupy themselves with solving conflicts like people because they do not spend time in a group. Snakes move forward most of the time and do not do the stop-starts which constrain action and forward momentum. Snakes have a sharp eye for observation like an eagle and would strike quickly when confronted by the enemy. Snakes would always go into a hole quickly and turn around in order to cast their eyes on the entrance to the hiding place because they are watchful. Individuals and organisations should always watch over their backs lest they are attacked unexpectedly.

The complete strategic action is epitomised in the mind of the crocodile. This reptile is a complete action packed monster which can fight on land and in the water. When the crocodile is relaxing in the sun it will open its mouth and flies find a comforting environment and fill up the monster's mouth; subsequently the crocodile will thankfully gobble the meal that offers itself while it is relaxing. If the crocodile faces an attack from the back on the land it can swing its tail and fatally strike the attacker. The tail of a crocodile is a powerful blade that can slice its prey and at the same time if attacked from the front it can grab and cut with its sharp teeth.

While the crocodile can fight on the land its main strength is in the water through applying the pull and drag motion by using its tail to lock the water and cannot be dragged out of the water. Oftentimes when the crocodile attacks from the water, it locks its jaws in the prey and drag the catch which cannot pull itself out of the water.

Decisive Strategic Action

As already alluded to in earlier submissions, action is critical for operationalising a strategy and realising results. In terms of the strategic thought process the action underpins the implementation stage of the strategy process. Decisive action demands that the timing and utilisation of time is right. Many great ideas of good intention if mistimed do not benefit the entity concerned. Great technological ideas mean nothing if they are not implemented the right time. Decisive action is therefore about relevance and impact on the objectives set out. The idea of acting decisively could be misconstrued to imply strolling through the park. Decisive action should be backed by resources and organisation to meet objectives. Action needs to be supported by resources.

In delivering learning as an academic for nearly thirty years I have come to understand that there are various resources that need to be in place in order to operationalise a strategy. Depending on the context and nature of the operation the different tasks take varying significance. The basic premise of a business model is driven by the 6Ms which are machinery, money, management, manpower, materials and minutes (time). Therefore great plans need great action to realise results through strategic impact.

The Personal Challenge

The call for strategic thinking and action is mandatory upon every person. Every day the jungle of life throws a challenge at us to harness and live. At a personal level everyone has issues to deal with and some of those issues are at the centre of life. In most cases when nations have good plans for their people the big task of strategizing to survive becomes minimal and many of us become free riders benefiting from national strategies where people live off the benefits of the state. If you flip a coin and cast your mind towards countries where national social welfare systems are alien survival becomes dog eat dog. The typical law of the jungle holds sway just like if the lion fails to outrun an antelope it is hunger and starvation and subsequent death or the reverse is true, that is where an antelope fails to outrun a lion and it is dinner for the lion.

We are therefore challenged as individuals to be fit to think and act decisively to win in the race for life. The call is for strength and focus in our spirit, soul and body. Some people excel in one or two aspects of the complete person and live skewed lives. You may have found an answer why some outstanding personalities with great athleticism and great body shape commit silly crimes or choose to demean their sexuality. A balanced life on handling the three key facets of a person are critical and a strategic mind should be natured to embrace a balanced approach to those issues.

Ultimately, whatever the circumstances a strategic mindset demands that we act on the opportunity. Robin Sharma puts it succinctly in saying that: "When you see an opportunity to change the world, get up and get the job done." We need to go beyond daydreaming and act like entrepreneurs who act on their dreams. It is imperative upon us to seek to be the example instead of trying to give examples of others whom we cannot be. What matters most is our belief in seeing it done and acting with our conscience. If our mindset is that situations present opportunities we remove one of the greatest impediments to progress; that is the problem mentality instead of seeing the field of opportunities. Great successes have not always been achieved by taking the easy path; hence we must be prepared for the difficult uphill climb that will take us to the top.

It is important to note that success is not an end game; instead success demands, adjusting the threshold of performance over time in view of the environmental dynamics. This necessitates reinvigorating and re-energizing efforts to remain on top of the game.

References

Adams, B. and Adams, C. (2000). "Transformation: Lead in times of change"., *Leadership Excellence*, p. 14 -15, February, 2000.

Bernoff, J. (2014). "Strategic Thinking for the Mobile Mind Shift". *Marketing News*, July 2014.

Brownlie, G. (1998) "High minds and low deeds: on being blind to creativity in strategic marketing.", Journal of Strategic Marketing (6), pp. 117-130.

Burke, R. (2006) "Leadership and spirituality"., *Foresight*, 8 (6) pp. 14-25.

Collins, J.C. and Porras, J.I. (1994), *Built to Last: Successful Habits of visionary companies.*, Harper Collins, New York.

Engel, B. (2007). "Eagle Soaring: The Power of the Resilient Self" *Journal of Psychosocial Nursing*, 45 (2), pp.44- 49.

Etzold, V. M. (2009),"St Paul as sales strategist: an essay commemorating the years of St Paul, 2008/2009", *Business Strategy Series*, Vol. 10 Iss: 2 pp. 86 – 89.

Haudan, J. (2000) "Great Management, It's more than just a promotion"., *Leadership Excellence*, p. 14, February, 2000.

Kadembo, E. M. (2016), "Story it! Brand it! Sell it!", Inspired Transformations Ltd, United Kingdom.

Kadembo, E.M. (2012). "Anchored in the story: The core of human understanding, branding, education, socialisation and the shaping of values". *The Marketing Review*, 12 (3), pp. 221-231.

Hyams-ssekasi, D. and Kadembo, E. M. (2013). "Leadership: A Question of the Brand". *International SAMANM Journal of Marketing and Management.*, 1(2), pp. 68-74.

Pellegrino, K.C. and Carbo, J.A. (2001), "Behind the mind of the Strategist", *The TQM Magazine*, 13 (6), pp. 375- 380.

Porter M., (2008). The five competitive forces that shape strategy. *Harvard Business Review*, 86 (1) pp. 78-93.

Peppard, M. (2010). "The Eagle and the Dove: Roman Imperial Sonship and the Baptism of Jesus (Mark 1: 9-11)". *New Testament Studies*, 56, pp. 431-45.

Wheatley, M. (2008). "Fearlessness: the last organisational change strategy", *Business executive*, August.

Woiceshyn, J. (2009). "Lessons from ''Good Minds'': How CEOs Use Intuition, Analysis and Guiding Principles to Make Strategic Decisions". *Long Range Planning* 42 pp. 298-319.

Online References

Gallo, C. http://www.forbes.com/sites#/sites/carminegallo/2011/01/04/the-7-success-principles-of-steve-jobs/ Accessed 22.10.2015

Online Learning for Sports Management, http://www.leoisaac.com/planning/strat016.htm, accessed, 03.08.16.